基本中國拳法

CHINESE GUNG FU
THE PHILOSOPHICAL ART OF
SELF DEFENSE

BY
BRUCE LEE

First Edition 1963
Second Edition 1987
Third Edition 1988
Manufactured in United States of America
Library of Congress Catalog Card Number:86-43242
ISBN 0-89750-112-8

Eighth printing 1993

WARNING

OHARA [ ] PUBLICATIONS, INCORPORATED
SANTA CLARITA, CALIFORNIA

DEDICATION

To my parents -

Mr.   and Mrs. Lee Hoi Chuen

and to my very good friend -

Mrs. Eva Tso

CONTENTS

- All drawings by Author -

ABOUT THE AUTHOR
By James Y. Lee

As mentioned before in my previous book, "Modern Kung Fu Karate", that the Brick Breaking and Iron Hand Training is not a necessary part of Gung Fu training - this book deals strictly with self defense.

Unlike my previous books on Gung Fu, written by one of limited knowledge, I was very happy when Mr. Bruce Lee was persuaded to come out with this, his first of a series of books on the Ancient Art of Gung Fu.

Bruce Lee, one of the highest authorities in the Chinese Art of Gung Fu in the United States today, came from China three years ago. At an early age, Mr. Lee started Gung Fu training from various instructors from both Northern and Southern schools of Gung Fu. At thirteen, he met Master Yip Man, leader of the Wing Chung School of Gung Fu, and since then he has devoted himself to that system. After years of daily training and engagements in competitive matches, he was awarded the rank of instructor - the youngest to achieve it in that school.

Since his arrival in the United States, Mr. Lee has selected a few disciples and devoted his time to teaching them. Among his many followers are Judo and Karate Black Belt holders, Gung Fu students of other systems, boxers, etc.

1

Aside from his knowledge of the various schools of Gung Fu, Mr. Lee is also well versed in Taoism and Ch'an (Zen). He has conducted a T.V. series in the U.S. on Oriental philosophy and Gung Fu.

Mr. Lee will be one who will bring credit to the ancient and noble art of Chinese Gung Fu by his sincere effort to present a true perspective of the art of Chinese self defense.

I was really impressed when in friendly sparring matches with Mr. Bruce Lee, I couldn't penetrate or land a telling blow or kick - even when he was blindfolded, once his hands are "sticking" to mine.

I am sure this book will bring to the citizens of the U.S. a better understanding of the principles which make Gung Fu such and effective system in defense. Students of other Oriental systems will benefit greatly from this book. In well illustrated photos, it clearly explains all the steps to master the various techniques.

Oscar Wilde once said, "Imitation is the most sincere compliment." If so, I have paid Mr. Bruce Lee a sincere compliment by changing all my Gung Fu techniques to his methods. When he demonstrated his type of striking, which is based on inner energy, I found it much more powerful than the power I had developed from previous Iron Hand training. The superiority of his Gung Fu is more refined and effective than that which I have learned in all my past years. Since his striking power is generated from the waist and the mind, I have always maintained that the power to break bricks is not the true test of actual application of energy in real combat.

I always benefit greatly whenever we get a chance to train together.

At present Mr. Lee, through his books, T. V. appearances and Gung Fu instructions to Americans, regardless of race, creed or national origin, is in the process of developing a nucleus of future Gung Fu instructors to keep the ancient Chinese art from being exploited and commercialized as evidenced unfortunately in some other Oriental systems.

I am in complete accord with the author when he says, "When more and more Americans are instructed in the authentic techniques of Gung Fu, less and less people will be able to pass themselves off as self styled Gung Fu "experts".

J. Y. Lee

ABOUT THE AUTHOR
By
Ed Parker

This is just a summation of my impressions as I observed Bruce Lee.

His system is unique, precise and extremely practical. Its principles and concepts are logical and basically sound. It is based on simplicity, but yet it is intricate; the movements are sticky but yet slippery, soft but yet firm, obvious but yet deceptive, dual but yet having oneness, angular but yet circular, not to mention the incredible speed and snap executed by Bruce Lee.

Not only is he highly adapt in his system, but as a conversationalist he is very interesting. His descriptive knowledge of other Chinese systems and their historical and philosophical background cannot help but make one an attentive listener.

He is one of the very few that I have seen who is gifted with natural ability, a gift which he undoubtedly has put to work evidenced by his superb skill.

I am glad to learn that he is writing books on Gung Fu. He confirms my faith in Gung-Fu and will be a great stimulant in present the art of Gung-Fu in its true and authentic light.

Publisher's Note: Mr. Parker is the well known Black Belt Kenpo Karate instructor of Pasadena, Calif., author of "Kenpo", owner of several Kenpo Karate studios.

4

"I highly recommend Mr. Bruce Lee's book on the Chinese Art of Gung Fu. This informative book will reveal an outstanding style of Chinese self defense. I have witnessed the teaching methods of the author and I find it concise and effective. I was also astonished with the vast knowledge this youthful Chinese Master possesses.

His "Wing Chung" system is unlike any other system of Gung Fu that I have seen. I have never seen anything like it.

I am convinced that this would be the system I would study if I were to begin my Gung Fu training again.

Master Bruce Lee, who is a gentleman, can actually apply his seemingly gentle method in actual application.

I have seen him perform with the grace and agility of a panther, and with lightning speed. He is truly a Master of a great style of Chinese fighting."

WALLY JAY
Head Instructor "Island Judo and Ju Jitsu" club, Alameda, California.
Black Belt 5th degree in Ju Jitsu - Black Belt 3rd degree in Kodakan Judo

INTRODUCTION

The center of the Far Eastern martial arts has been the art of Gung Fu, whose principles and techniques pervaded and influenced the different arts of Oriental self-defense. Because Gung Fu has been shrouded under a veil of utmost secrecy, it is very seldom heard of in the Western world as well as many other Far Eastern countries.

Its history covers four thousand years. At first in the midst of antiquity, Gung Fu was simply a no-holds-barred type of fighting, but as the centuries went by, countless generations of its practitioners gradually perfected it, smoothing out the rough spots, polishing the techniques, until it began to emerge as something definitely superior. Later on, the studies of anatomy, religions, psychology are included, and Gung Fu advanced one more step to a highly scientific and philosophical type of self-defense. That was around two or three thousand years ago! Gung Fu is for health promotion, cultivation of mind, and self-protection. Its philosophy is based on the integral parts of the philosophies of Taoism (道學), Ch'an (Zen 禪) and I'Ching (Book of Changes 易經 — the ideal of giving with adversity, to bend slightly and spring back stronger than before, and to adapt oneself harmoniously to the opponent's movements without striving or resisting. The techniques of Gung Fu emphasize not on power but in conservation of energy and moderation without going to either extreme (Yin & Yang 陰陽). That is why a true Gung Fu man never opposes force (which will create reaction) or give way completely; he is simply pliable, as a spring. He seeks to merge harmoniously <u>with</u> the oncoming force of the opponent -- to be the complement, and not the opposite of the opponent's force.

It has been quite a number of years that I have indulged myself in Wing Chuing, the School of Artlessness; my mind is no longer distracted by the opponent, "self", or formal techniques, etc. I have made my opponent's techniques my techniques; my task is simply to complete the other half of the "oneness", and my action is that of Wu-Wei (spontaneous act) which is according to the circumstances without pre-arrangement. The training of mind and imagination, imagination and Ch'i (breath), breath and energy, etc., are all gone. There is nothing to "try" to do; everything simply flows.

Now I am asked, by a very good friend of mine, to write a book on Gung Fu techniques, which I have long forgotten. In order to fulfill his wish, I have included here in this book some of the basic techniques of the various schools of Gung Fu I have learned before my joining the school of Wing Chuing. It is true that the mental aspect in Gung Fu is the desired end; however, in order to achieve this stage, technical skill of the art has to come first.

I like to stress that this is not a text book on Gung Fu formal techniques; rather, it is a book on some of the basic blocking and striking in that art. In the very near future, after my trip back from the Orient, a more thorough book entitled "The Tao of Chinese Gung Fu" will be published.

Since my three years stay in the U.S. I've seen unscrupulous "business men", Americans and Chinese alike, who claim themselves professors or masters of Gung Fu, and whose movements resemble nothing to any school in Gung Fu. I hope that people who are about to

7

join these schools will examine closely. I also like to add that whoever reads this book will not be able to become a "holy terror"; nor can he be a Gung Fu expert in just three easy lessons.

B. Lee

CHINESE MARTIAL ART

The Chinese Martial Art basically consists of five "ways":

1 - Striking
(打法)
- Includes all techniques of palms, fists, knees, elbows, shoulders, fore-arms, head, thighs (does not include different school's special techniques like the eagle claws, the beak of the crane, the mantis hand, etc.)

2 - Kicking
(踢法)
- Includes all types of techniques of kicking (both northern and schools of China.)

3 - Joint Locks
(橋拿)
- Seventy-two techniques of different joint breaking and locking.

4 - Throwing
(摔法)
- Thirty-six techniques of throwing.

5 - Weapons
(武器)
- Eighteen different weapons.

There are innumerable schools of Gung Fu in both Northern and Southern parts of China. Among some of the well known schools are:

In Northern China: - Wing Chung School (詠春派 八卦), Bart Kuar Clan (形意), Ying Yee ( ), N. Praying Mantis (螳螂), Eagle Claw School 鷹爪派), Tam Tuei (譚腿門), Springing Leg (彈腿門), Northern Sil Lum (北少林), Law Hon (羅漢拳), Lost Track School (迷踪藝), Wa K'ung (西嶽華拳 Ch'a K'ung (查拳), Monkey Style (猴拳) 大聖門), Chuiang Kung P'ai (長江派), etc.

<u>In Southern China</u>: - Wing Chung School (詠春派), Southern Praying Mantis (南派螳螂), Dragon Style (白眉派), White Crane School (白鶴派), Northern Sil Lum (南派少林), Choy Lay Fut (蔡李佛), Hung K'ung (洪家), Choy Ga (蔡家), Fut Ga (佛家), Mok Ga (莫家), Yal Gung Moon (柔功門), Li Ga (李家), Lau Ga (劉家), etc.

Then these clans are separated into so-called internal and external schools (內家与外家). Here we are not concerned with them.

Several Important Pointers

1.   Every movement of Gung Fu has a flowing continuity without any dislocation. As soon as a movement is completed, it begins to flow into another one. Because of this the readers will find the techniques of Gung Fu faster than the ordinary method.

2.   Gung Fu is a mind exercise. The combination of mind and body is especially important in the higher stage of Gung Fu. As for the reader here, try to use the imagination (mental movement) to influence every physical movement; for example, a firm belief that every technique will come to the desired end would help.

3.   Cooperate with your opponent. Do not resist or interrupt his flow of movement. Instead of stopping his force, complete it by following him. In other words, you help him to destroy himself. Remember this - what you will do depends on your opponent; that is why we say - be the complement and not the opposite of the opponent's force.

4.   The waist is very important in the art of Gung Fu, as it plays a major part in both striking and dissolving away the opponent's force. During practice, the practitioner is required to dissolve away the opponent's force by turning waist first before he can side step it. (Note: A white arrow will show the direction of turning of the waist in the illustration.

5.   Remember - it is better to learn how to endure than to learn how to fight. However, if you are compelled to oppose force, make use of it.

BASIC GUNG FU STANCES

Gung Fu has many stances for different purposes, and some other schools have their own
special stances. Here are the ten most commonly used stances for the beginners.

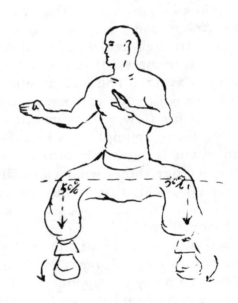

1 - Ma Bo (　馬 步　) - The thighs must be para-
　　　llel, the toes point front, and the knees
　　　point at the toes. The nearer the dis-
　　　tance of the feet, the better.
　　　Points to Avoid - Standing bow-legged
　　　or leaning forward or backward.

2 - Gung Bo (弓 步) - The weight is on the front
      leg with toes pointed slightly inward
      (avoid being stepped on); the back leg
      straight. (This is why this is some-
      times called the bow's arrow stance.
      This stance and Ma Bo (horse stance)
      are strong and firm stances.
      <u>Points to Avoid</u> - Lifting the heel up on
      back foot, or pointing toes straight front
      on the front foot.

3 - Ding Bo (丁 步) - Most of the weight is on
the back leg, the front leg stands with
toe pointing (ready to kick any time).
The front knee is slightly higher than
the back one for protection of the
private part.
Points to Avoid - Weight on front leg,
toes not pointing straight.

4 - Hui Bo (鹿 步) - A slight variation of Ding
        Bo, except with front toes turned
        slightly inward.
        Points to Avoid - Weight on front foot.

5 - Chung Sik (中 式) - This is a medium stance
between Ma Bo and Hui Bo, and is
mostly used in free-style sparring, due
to its flexibility. The front knee is
slightly higher than the rear one.

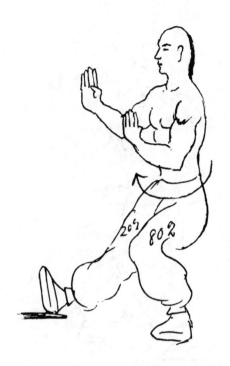

6 - Chuat Sing (七 星) - Weight on back leg, the
front leg rests lightly on heel with toes
pointing upward. This is mostly used
with Gung Bo for dissolving away force.
The waist plays a very important part
in this stance. Both knees try to be
parallel.

602

402

7 - Lau Ma (摟 馬) - The twisting horse. The
  front foot flat on ground with the back
  heel raised. This stance is used mostly
  in close-range for moving with the
  shortest time.

8 - Kuai Ma (跪 馬) - The weight is on the front kneeing leg. This stance is used mostly for the attack to the low gate.

9 - Tou Bo (偷 步) - This stance in English
means to steal a step, to sneak in to
attack.   From this stance one can
either kick or change it to many other
stances like Ma Bo, Ding Bo, Gung Bo,
etc.

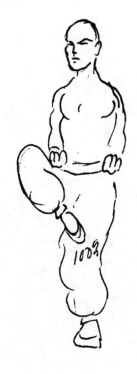

- Tu Ma (吊 馬) - In English, hanging horse, this stance is for defense against foot sweeps, low kicks, weapon attacks, etc. From this position, a kick is often connected.

THE SEVEN STARS

Watch for the opponent's seven parts

1) hands
2) feet
3) elbows
4) knees
5) shoulders
6) thighs
7) head

THE THREE FRONTS

Take care of one's "three fronts"

1) in front of one's eyes

2) in front of one's hands

3) in front of one's legs

ON WAIST TRAINING

The waist plays a vital role in the art of Gung Fu. Here are some exercises to extend the range of its motion and make the waist flexible.

Fig. 1 - Front Bend
(1) Bend forward with palms touching ground, (2) legs keep straight at all times.

Fig. 2
(1) Bend forward and grasp both ankles and touch head on the knees.

(2) Later on the head should touch the shin or, even better, the instep.

Fig. 3 - Side Bend
(1) Body turn left and bend down without moving the lower trunk,

(2) Touch palms on ground,

(3) Come up and repeat the same to the right side.

Fig. 4 to Fig. 6 - Back Bend
Figures 4 to 6 show the steps toward back bending.

Fig. 6
Stand with feet together, hand naturally raised, body twisted toward left side (Fig. 6a); (2) The body turns from left toward right (Fig. 6b); (3) Right hand turns to a hook and left hand, following the turning of the waist, drops down and grasps right ankle (Fig. 6c); (4) Left hand releases and turn body from right to left again.

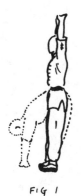

FIG 1

FIG 2

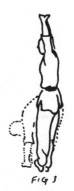

FIG 3

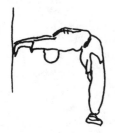

FIG 4

FIG 5

FIG 6

Fig. 7

(1) From the standing position the body drop toward the right side with right foot crossing in front of left foot (Fig. 7a);

(2) Body turns backward with left foot grinding the ground, and right foot slightly touching ground (Fig. 7b);

(3) After turning left foot bends slightly on the knee.

Fig. 8

(1) Assume squatting position as in Fig. 8a with left foot in front; the chest is close to the knee.

(2) Body turns toward right back with hand following (Fig. 8b).

(3) After turning the waist, the right leg should be in front as in Fig. 8b, dotted lines.

(4) Ready for left turning.

FIG 6 A

FIG 6 B

FIG 6 C

FIG 7 A

FIG 7 B

FIG 8 A

FIG 8 B

ON LEG TRAINING

The kick, especially to the Northern clans of Gung Fu, is a best means of attack; however, they too warn the danger of using them recklessly. It is a fact that the legs are much more powerful and have a longer reach than the hands, but we must consider also that when we lift one leg and kick, our whole balance is involved.

"In training, kick as high as you can; but in combat, kick as fast as you can and don't pass over the belt." This is a saying I often teach to my students. In my school, our kicks seldom pass over the belt, and the so called high or flying kicks are never used. As for leg training, and this is true in most of the Gung Fu schools (North or South), it is not necessary for us to strengthen and toughen it by kicking on hard objects or sandbags. Due to their support of the whole body everyday, our legs already have power, and it is a matter of cultivating them naturally. The training then involves the cultivating and concentrating of power, and the development of speed.

Here I have included a few basic exercises that serve to develop the kicking; the first part of which will concentrate on stretching the ligaments and extending the range of motion. The second part will be the natural development of kicking power.

Fig. 1 (Front Bend)

Assume the position in Fig. 1 with hands on right knee to prevent it from bending. With the toes raised, try to touch the knee with your head. Repeat 15 times on each leg.

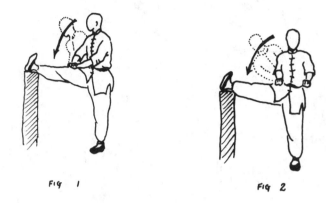

Fig. 1   Fig. 2

Fig. 2 (Side Bend)

Assume position in Fig. 2 with hand on hip. With toes raised, bend sideways and touch the right foot with your head.

Fig 3A   Fig 3B

Fig. 3A - This exercise is commonly called shoe kissing. (1) Assume a squatting position with left leg extending straight, toes raised and the heel touching the ground, (2) with two hands grasping left foot and pulling backward, bend forward and kiss the shoe (fig. 3B). Practice left and right. NOTE: At first, practice by touching the head on knees, then reach farther and farther out.

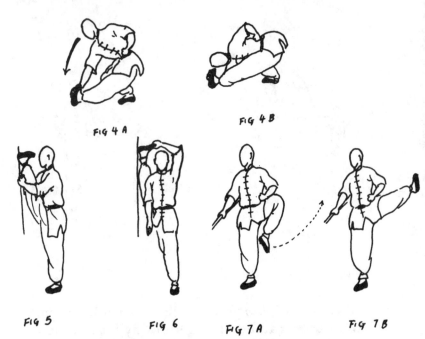

FIG 4 A

FIG 4 B

FIG 5

FIG 6

FIG 7 A

FIG 7 B

Fig. 4 A- Assume same position, but this time
bend over and try to touch shoe with
the head. (This time the right side of
the body touches the left leg.) Repeat
12-20 times and do the same with right
leg.

Fig. 5 & Fig. 6
Fig. 5 and Fig. 6 show a slight but more
difficult exercise of leg training.

Fig. 7A- Side Hang. This exercise is known as
leg hanging in Chinese because when the
leg is raised to the desired position, it
has to stop there for as long as one can.
(1) Assume position A in Fig. 7A with
right hand on a bar, (2) Slowly lift left
Fig. 7B- leg (with toes raised) to around 90° from
the ground and stay there for a while,
(3) Lower down to original position and
repeat the same procedure again.

Fig. 8A- Straight Hang.
   (1) Assume original position, (2) This
   time, instead of raising the leg sideways, raise it slowly straight up (toe
Fig. 8B- raised) till it reaches at least 90° from
   ground, (3) Stay there for a while and
   repeat again.

FIG 8 A   FIG 8 B   FIG 9

Fig. 9 - This is front high kick for practising
   purposes only. (1) With hands on hips
   advance right foot with left foot behind
   it, (2) Left foot kick up straight with
   toes raised aiming at one's forehead.
   (3) When left foot comes down next to
   right foot, stop and advance left foot
   with right foot behind, ready to kick.
   NOTE: (1) During kicking the waist
          should not bend, and do not
          lean forward too much.
          (2) The body should not bend
          backward.
          (3) The stationary foot should
          be firmly flat on the ground.

Fig. 10 - Side Slanting Kick
      (1) Assume same position as in Fig. 9
and kick with left leg the same way
except to the side of right ear.
(2) The hand extending position is for
balancing the posture of the body.

Fig. 11 - Side Straight Kick
      (1) From erect position advance right
foot with toes slightly pointing to the
right side; body also turned toward
right side as shown in Fig. 11.
(2) Left foot kick toward left ear,
(3) Left foot lands on ground with toes
pointing slightly toward left side and
body turning left side.   (4) Kick in the
same manner.

Figs. 12, 13, 14
      (1) Fig. 12 and Fig. 14 show the exer-
cise of leg swinging of out and inward
swing.   Practise with left and right.
(2) Fig. 13 shows the correct posture
while swinging the leg.

Fig. 15- This is the actual kicking as used in
actual application.   Here I have just
included three basic kicks in Gung Fu,
the straight-toe and thrust kick, and
the side kick.
(1) Assume position in Fig. 15 with body
erect, (2) Advance right foot and snap
out left foot like a whip with all the
power concentrating on impact, (3) Snap
back as fast as possible and land in front
of right foot, (4) In the same manner the
right foot snaps out.

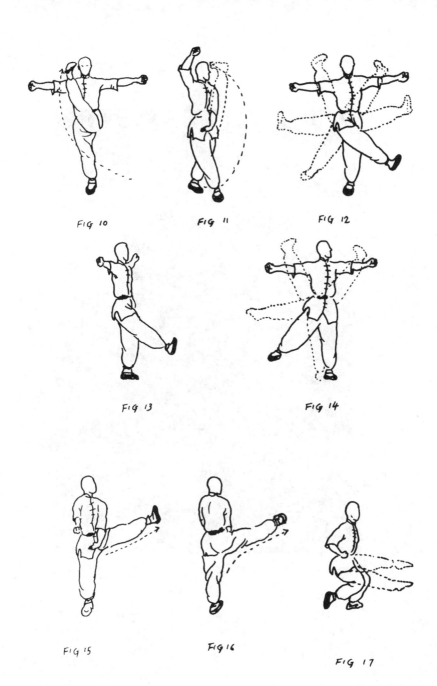

FIG 10

FIG 11

FIG 12

FIG 13

FIG 14

FIG 15

FIG 16

FIG 17

33

CHINESE GUNG FU

THE PHILOSOPHICAL ART OF

SELF DEFENSE

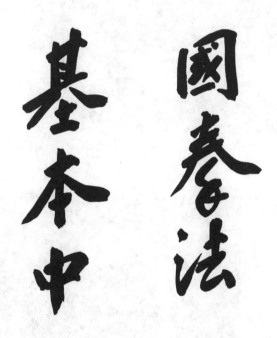

1-A

1-B

36

1-C

1-A   A comes in with straight left punch in Gung
       Bo (弓 步 - Bow and Arrow stance).

1-B   Turning his waist, B dissolves A's punch
       in an upward arc. Unlike other schools of
       blocking with power, Gung Fu block tends
       to dissolve the oncoming force and return
       it back to the opponent. (Notice white ar-
       row indicate the direction of turning of the
       waist.)

1-C   Continuing his motion B follows with fingers
       job to attacker's eye. Notice the other hand
       is on guard. (Note - After constant practice
       the blocking and striking should be one con-
       tinuous action.

37

2-A

2-B

2-C

2-A   A leads with straight left.

2-B   B steps in with Chung Sik (中 式 medium
       stance), simultaneously deflects the punch
       with left slapping hand (左拍手), and
       strikes opponent with right knuckle fist
       (右插捶).

2-C   A thrusts out his right, and B, without
       changing his position, blocks it with his left
       and at the same time jabs A's throat with
       upward finger poke from where his right
       hand was (右插喉掌).

3-A

3-B

3-A   A leads with right punch

3-B   At the slightest movement of A, B steps
        back, blocks and side kicks opponent at the
        same time (　右側撑腿　). (Notice
        right hand is in position.)

4-A

4-B

4-C

4-A   A comes in with right hook.

4-B   B side steps and, turning his waist, blocks and jabs opponent's eyes simultaneously.

4-C   A again comes in with left upper cut to mid-section. B side steps and at the same time slashes down his right and again jabs A with left finger thrusts (標 指).

5-A

5-B

44

5-C

5-A   A grasps B's both hands.

5-B   B advances right foot and at the same time
       strikes A's right wrist bone by his own left
       thumb.

5-C   After A releases the grip, B then punches
       his face with a straight right (冲捶).

6-A

6-B

6-A   A bear-hug from the rear. B relaxes and
           sinks down his weight.

6-B   Turning his waist, B strikes A with his
           elbow and at the same time steps on his
           toes.

7-A   A comes in with straight-right in left Gung
       Bo.

7-B B side steps, deflects the punch, and strikes A's ribs with knuckle fist (插 捶).

8-A   A comes in with right side kick (右側撐腿)

8-B   B comes down (in an arc) with hand hook
      (notice left hand is on guard) and counters
      by kicking A's groin with straight toe kick.
      (　直挑腿　)

9-A

9-B

52

9-C

9-A   A pushes B.

9-B   B, turning his waist and advancing, deflects
       and strikes A with knuckle fist (　搨捶　)
       as shown in the picture.

9-C   Turning his right hand in an arc to lead the
       oncoming movement of the opponent, B
       skips in and strikes him with the knee.

10-A

10-B

10-C

10-A, B   A comes in with lunging straight right
          punch.

10-C   Without backing, B turns his waist and
          leads the opponent to the direction of his
          own movement.

10-D A intends to pull each right punch and snap out his left.

10-E   At the slightest movement of withdrawal,
       B follows and slaps down and locks A's
       both arms; at the same time, B strikes A
       with a straight right.

11-A

11-B

11-C

11-A, B   A intends to throw B as shown in picture
          A & B. (There are, by the way, 36
          throwing techniques and 72 joint locks in
          the art of Gung Fu.)

11-C   Turning his waist, B grasps A's left
          hand and at the same time turns his
          shoulder out and downward against A's
          shoulder.

11-D

11-E

11-D, E   By kicking his right foot sharply into a
Gung Bo, B counters A by throwing him.
(Knee or fist can follow to finish opponent.)

12-A

12-A   Opponent A steps in with straight finger jab.

12-B   Without backing, B leads A's force by turning his waist, and at the same time strikes A with the edge of the hand.

(Acknowledgement: Mr. Charles Woo, the defender, by the way, is a 2nd degree black belt Judo holder.)

13-A   A leads with straight right. B deflects
        by right hand. (Notice left hand on guard.)

13-B   A withdraws right and shoots out his left
to mid-section. B simply slaps the punch
downward with left and jabs A's eyes with
his right from previous position.

14-A   A comes in with left. B deflects the punch with right hand hook.

14-B   A withdraws his left and shoots out his
        right. B deflects the oncoming punch with
        left hand (in the form of an arc) and, fol-
        lowing A's withdrawal of energy, he strikes
        A with right knuckle fist (from the previous
        hooking position).

15-A

15-B

5-A, B   Right at this moment X doesn't concentrate
on any of his opponent's actions, he simply
has a quiet awareness of the immediate
situation without thinking of the outcome or
anything. Opponent, A, attacks X with right
hook. X, turning his waist, blocks and jabs
A with right. (Notice the changing of foot
work.)

15-C

15-B, C   As X disables A, B comes in with a straig
punch. From where he is, X turns his
waist, deflects and side kicks B.

15-D

15-C, D   At this moment C lunges in with straight
right to the face. X dissolves the punch in
an arc and at the same time strikes him with
a knuckle fist.

16-A

16-B

16-C

16-A, B   A steps in with right straight heart punch. X deflects the punch and counters with back fist (掛捶 to A's temple. At this moment B comes in.

16-B, C   X sweeps his left back in an arc and slides in with kneeing horse and strikes B's groin as shown in the picture.

17-A   A comes in with straight knuckle fist to solar plexus.

17-B

17-A, B   B, turning his waist, hooks A's punch
and counters with straight knuckle fist.

18-A

18-B

18-A   A & B facing in ready position.

18-A, B   A comes in with finger jab to B's throat.
B leads A's movement by turning his
waist. This dissolving is not by the
hand, but by the waist so as to really
unbalance the oncoming force as he
makes it.

19-A

19-B

19-C

19-A A and B in natural position. As A applies pressure on B's hand.

19-B B assists A by jerking him to the direction of his force, and at the same time skips in with a straight thrust kick. (Notice the left hand is in position.)

19-B, C A blocks B's straight kick with his left. B, by following the direction of A's blocking, turns and kicks A's knee with a low side thrust kick.

THE BASIC THEORY OF YIN AND YANG
IN THE ART OF GUNG FU

At first I did not plan to include this section as the book deals only with basic techniques; however, on second thought, I believe the reader will be greatly benefited by this Chinese view of life. Most likely his technique (no matter what system he is in) will also be greatly improved.

The basic structure of Gung Fu is based on the theory of Yin/Yang (陰 陽), a pair of mutually complementary forces that act continuously, without cessation, in this universe. This Chinese way of life can be applied to anything, but here we are interested in its relationship to the art of Gung Fu. The black part of the circle is called Yin (陰). Yin can represent anything in the universe as:

negativeness, passiveness, gentleness, insubstantiality, femaleness, moon, darkness, night, etc. The other complementary part of the circle is Yang (陽), which represents positiveness, activeness, firmness, substantiality, maleness, sun, brightness, day, etc.

The common mistake most people make is to identify this Yin/Yang symbol, T'ai-Chi (太 極), as dualistic; that is Yang being the opposite of Yin, and vice versa. As long as we separate this "oneness" into two, we won't achieve realization. Actually, all things have their complementary part; it is only in the human mind and his perception that

80

they are being separated into opposites. The sun
is not the opposite of the moon, as they complement and are interpendent on each other, and we
cannot survive without either of them. In a similar way, a male is but the complement of the
female; for without the male, how on earth do
we know there is female, or vice versa. The
"one-ness" of Yin/Yang is necessary in life. If
a person riding a bicycle wishes to go somewhere,
he cannot pump on both the pedals at the same
time or not pumping on them at all. In order to
move forward, he has to pump one pedal and re-
lease the other. So the movement of going forward requires this "oneness' of pumping and releasing. Pumping then is the result of releasing,
and vice versa; each being the cause of the other.

In the Yin/Yang symbol there is a white spot
on the black part, and a black spot on the white
one.   This is to illustrate the balance
in life, for nothing can survive long by going to
either extremes, be it negativeness or positive-
mess. Therefore, firmness must be concealed
in gentleness, and gentleness in firmness, and
that is why a Gung Fu man must be pliable as a
spring. Notice that the stiffest tree is most eas-
ily cracked, while the bamboo or will bend with
the wind. So in Gung Fu, or any other system,
one must be gentle yet not giving away completely; be firm yet not hard, and even if he is strong,
he should guard it with softness and tenderness.
For if there is no softness in firmness, he is not
strong; in a similar way, if one has firmness
concealed in softness, no one can break through
his defense. This principle of moderation pro-
vides a best means of preserving oneself, for
since we accept this existence of the one-ness
(Yin/Yang) in everything, and do not treat it du-
alistically, we thus secure a state of tranguility

by remaining detached and not inclining to either extreme. Even if we do incline on one extreme, be it negative or positive, we will flow with it in order to control it. This flowing with it without clinging is the true way to get rid of it.

When the movements in Yin/Yang flow into extremes, reaction sets in. For when Yang goes to the extreme, it changes to Yin; and when Yin (activated by Yang) goes to the extreme, it returns back to Yang (that is why each one is the result and cause of the other.) For example, when one works to the extreme, he becomes tired and has to rest (from Yang to Yin). After resting, he can work again (Yin back to Yang). This incessant changing of Yin/Yang is always continuous.

The application of the theory of Yin/Yang in Gung Fu is known as the Law of Harmony, in which one should be in harmony with, and not against the force of the oponent. Suppose A applies strength on B, B shouldn't oppose or gives way completely to it. For these are but the two extreme opposites of B's reaction. Instead, he should complete A's force, with a lesser force, and lead him to the direction of his own movement. As the butcher preserves his knife by cutting along the bone and not against it, a Gung Fu man preserves himself by following the movement of his opponent without opposition or even striving (Wu-wai 無为 spontaneous, or spirit action). This spontaneous assisting of A's movement as he aims it will result in his own defeat.

When a Gung Fu man finally understood the theory of Yin/Yang, he no longer "fusses" with so-called "gentleness" or "firmness"; he simply does what the moment requires him to do. In fact, all conventional forms and techniques are all gone, his movements are those of everyday movements. He doesn't have to "justify" himself like so many other masters have, claiming his spirit or his internal power; to him' cultivation of martial art in the long run will return to simplicity, and only people of half-way cultivation justify and brag about themselves.

Bruce Lee
Oakland, California

DIFFERENCE IN GUNG FU STYLE

The techniques of a superior system of Gung Fu is based on simplicity. It is only the half cultivated systems that are full of and unnecessary wasted motions.

Simplicity is the natural result of profound and long study of the "way" of movements. A good Gung Fu man is a simplifier.

Here are some examples of a slower system against the more effective Gung Fu techniques.

Fig. 100   "A" advances with "pow chuie", uppe cut blow.

Fig. 101   "B", without wasted motions, simply hooks down with his left hand and strikes "A"s carotid artery by following his withdrawing energy.

85

Fig. 200   In **Gung Fu** one never grabs some-
one **as shown.** For illustration, let's
as sume **that** "B" grabs "A"s clothing.

Fig. 200   "A" advances right foot and attempts
right upward elbow stroke.
It is dangerous to use the elbow
in far range - as you can see during
"A"s advance, "B" can simply punch
straight (Fig. 201). Elbows should
be reserved for close range combat.

Fig. 202   "B" continues the action and throws
"A" with cross hock throw, and simultaneously strikes "A"s jaw with heel
of hand blow.

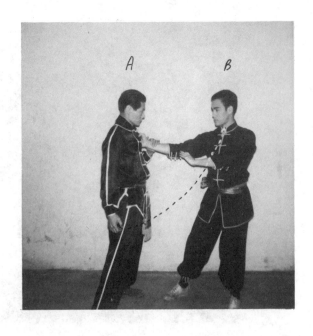

201

202

87

Fig. 300   When grabbed by somebody, instead
            of applying joint lock or pushing him
            off-balance, one is better off by
            simply kicking his attacker on the
            shin, or if his other hand is free,
            just punch him.

            Let's assume B grabs A's hand
            and A tries to unbalance B's posture
            by advancing his right foot and at
            the same time pushing B's elbow to-
            ward his own body. (Fig. 3A)

Fig. 301   During the process of all these
            movements B can either kick A's
            groin while he advances, or just
            jab at his eye. Or, as shown on
            Figure 301, comes in with both
            hand jab and toe kick.

Fig. 400   A grasps B's hand and pulls him
            in for the left side elbow to ribs.

Fig. 401   B simply drops his elbow and,
            following in an arc facing A, strikes
            him at the same time with his left
            finger jab. A straight kick can be
            followed.

400

401

Fig. 500   B comes in with straight right and A, in twisting horse, deflects B's punch.

Fig. 501   Advancing into a horse stance slightly toward the right side of B, A is ready for a side hand chop to B's ribs. Actually B can now come in by a finger jab or edge of the hand by checking A's elbow with left hand.

Fig. 502   As A comes in B, in the same position all the time, deflects the punch with right hand and counters with a right hook kick. (Fig. 5C)

501

502

93

The following are some photos taken at Ralph Castro's Kenpo Karate Studio in San Francisco, California, during a recent visit.

Author and Ed Parker in "Bi Jong" or "ready position"

Front Row - Author Bruce Lee, James Lee
Back Row - Ed Parker, Ralph Castro, Black
Belt Kenpo Karate instructors.

Author with Ed Parker and James Lee during Gung Fu gabfest.

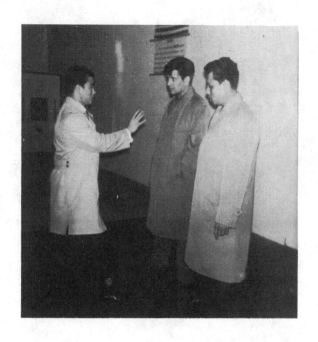

Author, Ed Parker and Ralph Castro. Note Castro's spacious studio.

Bruce Lee's Fighting Method
Skill in Techniques
Volume 3
by Bruce Lee and M. Uyehara

To help the student refine and polish his self-defense techniques as well as make use of the well-conditioned body, Bruce Lee teaches how to develop skills in body movement, in hand techniques, kicking, parrying, striking vital target points, and sparring. Lee also compares the classical methods of hand techniques and parrying with the methods of jeet kune do and clarifies the differences. Illustrated.

Bruce Lee's Fighting Method
Advanced Techniques
Volume 4
by Bruce Lee and M. Uyehara

Intended primarily for the student who has already availed himself of the first three volumes, Bruce Lee presents the advanced techniques of his fighting method. All fully illustrated, chapters include: Hand Techniques for Offense Attacks With Kicks, Defense and Counter, and Attributes and Tactics, which includes a comparison of the mechanical versus the intelligent fighter.

Code No. 404
Size 6″ x 9″, 128 pages

Code No. 405
Size 6″ x 9″, 128 pages

Write to: **Ohara Publications, Inc.**
24715 Avenue Rockefeller, P.O. Box 918, Santa Clarita, California 91380-9018

Tao of Jeet Kune Do
by Bruce Lee

After intensive study of different martial arts styles and theories, Bruce Lee developed a concept of martial arts for the individual man which he labeled *jeet kune do*, the way of the intercepting fist. This international best-seller explains the philosophic basis of jeet kune do in the original words and drawings of the late martial artist and film star himself. Lee's views on Zen, physical training, combat, martial virtues and failings, and many other topics are all presented here. In *Tao of Jeet Kune Do* Lee integrates his philosophy of martial arts with his philosophy of living.

Code No. 401
Size 8½" x 11", 208 pages

The Legendary Bruce Lee
by the Editors of BLACK BELT magazine

This book is a collection of articles detailing the life of Bruce Lee, from his childhood in Hong Kong to his rise to superstar status. Written at various times during Lee's career, these articles trace his development as a martial artist, from wing chun practitioner, student of Yip Man, to the founding of jeet kune do. The philosophy and techniques of his art are explained by an article written by Lee himself, and in interviews conducted in his Chinatown school. His work in the movies is also covered, the centerpiece being an article written by his wife Linda Lee about the making of the movie *Way of the Dragon*. Friends and fellow martial artists, including many celebrities, tell of their involvement with Lee and the effect he had on their lives. This book features scores of photographs showing both the public and private sides of this enigmatic superstar.

Code No. 446
Size 6" x 9", 160 pages

Write to: **Ohara Publications, Inc.**
24715 Avenue Rockefeller, P.O. Box 918, Santa Clarita, California 91380-9018

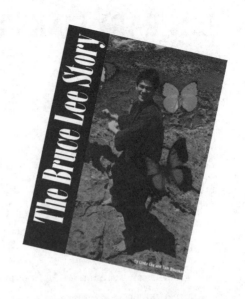

THE BRUCE LEE STORY

by Linda Lee
with Tom Bleecker

Like a meteor, Bruce Lee flashed
brilliantly through the world of martial arts and motion pictures. Then,
on July, 20, 1973, like a meteor he
vanished—extinguished by sud-
den death at age 32. Here is the
complete story of the legendary
martial artist/actor Bruce Lee . . .
by the person who knew him best
—his wife, Linda Lee. Through his
movies and books, Bruce Lee is still
introducing the martial arts to people all over the world more than 15
years after his death. This is the
no-holds-barred story of Bruce Lee.
Code No. 460
Size 8-1/4" x 10-1/4", 192 pages

Write to: **Ohara Publications, Inc.**
24715 Avenue Rockefeller, P.O. Box 918, Santa Clarita, California 91380-9018

LITERARY LINKS TO THE ORIENT

OHARA ⓟ PUBLICATIONS, INCORPORATED

24715 Avenue Rockefeller, P.O. Box 918, Santa Clarita, California 91380-9018